WALLY, THE LOST BABY WALRUS

ISBN 1-888125-59-4

Library of Congress Catalog Card Number:99-067082

Chris Kiana Sr., MBA

Publication Consultants

PO Box 221974 Anchorage, Alaska 99522-1974 email alaskaod@alaska.net

Illustrated by
Minnie Kiana Morken

Once upon a time, Wally the baby walrus was swimming with his mother.

They swam along near the bottom of the ocean.

They had gotten lost from the main walrus herd.

Wally's mother slowed down.

She rested in the water.

An airplane flew high over them.

Mamma walrus swam slowly to a small island.

Soon, they were on the island.

Wally's mother lay down to rest.

She would never move again.

Mamma walrus had joined her ancestors.

Wally stayed with her until he got hungry.

Wally was still hungry

He swam toward
an Eskimo village.

He was very tired and hungry.

Wally crawled onto the beach tired from his swim.

He felt all alone in the world.

The baby walrus rested for now.

Wally soon heard the loud roar of an airplane.

He looked up at the airplane.

The airplane was high in the sky.

The pilot of the airplane saw Wally.

He called the radio
operator at the airport.

"There is something on
the runway," he said.

The jet airplane landed next
to Wally on the runway.

The lost baby walrus looked all around the busy airport.

But all Wally could think of now was food.

Airport guards came out to take a look.

They found poor little tired and hungry Wally.

They chased him away from the runway.

Someone brought a blanket
to the guards.

They put poor
little tired
Wally into it.

The guards carried him to the airport office.

Wally was scared.

They put him down outside the airport office.

A guard brought him food to eat.

Another guard
brought him
milk to drink.

He was
so hungry
and thirsty.

Wally ate
and drank.

He was too
busy eating
and drinking to
be scared anymore

Wally soon went to sleep in his new home.

An airport guard watched over him.

He had just been through a bad time.

Wally soon found that he had some new friends.

His friends played with him and fed him.

They all had a good time.

One day Wally crawled down to the beach.

He found a seagull.

The bird let him come close.

Wally greeted the seagull with a grunt.

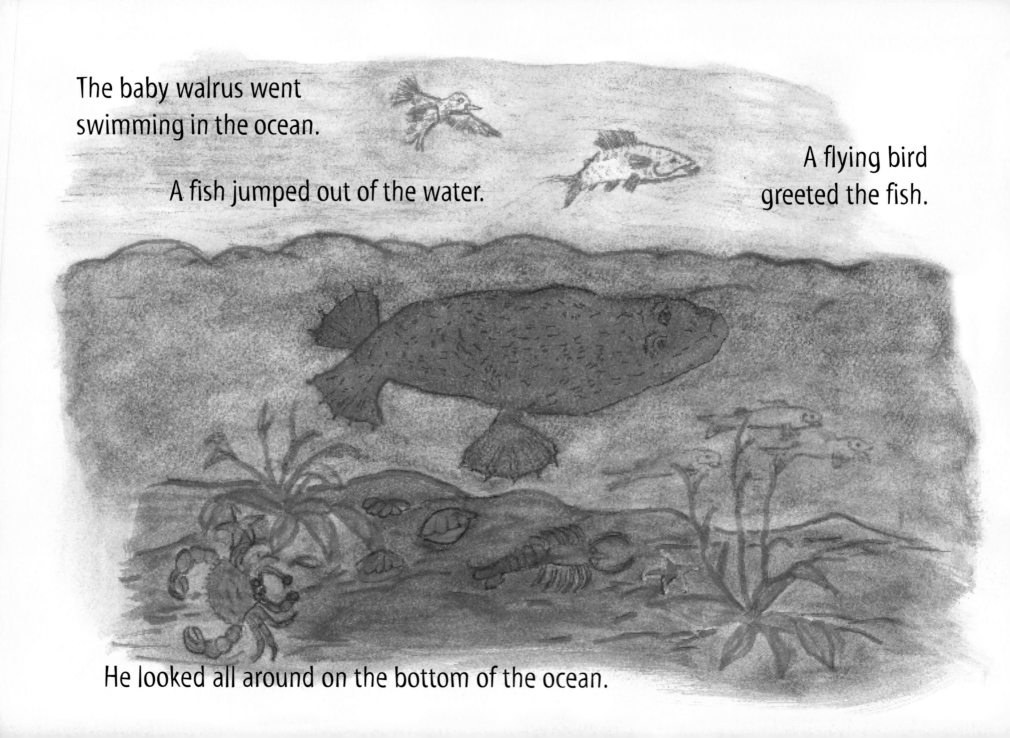

The baby walrus went swimming in the ocean.

A fish jumped out of the water.

A flying bird greeted the fish.

He looked all around on the bottom of the ocean.

Wally was resting on a piece of floating ice.

He saw a salmon jump out of the water next to him.

Wally was happy once again.

All was well with Wally.

Wally went
 swimming again.

He stopped to look at
an underwater plant.

The baby walrus liked
everything
he saw.

Wally swam on.

He was joined by a school of fish.

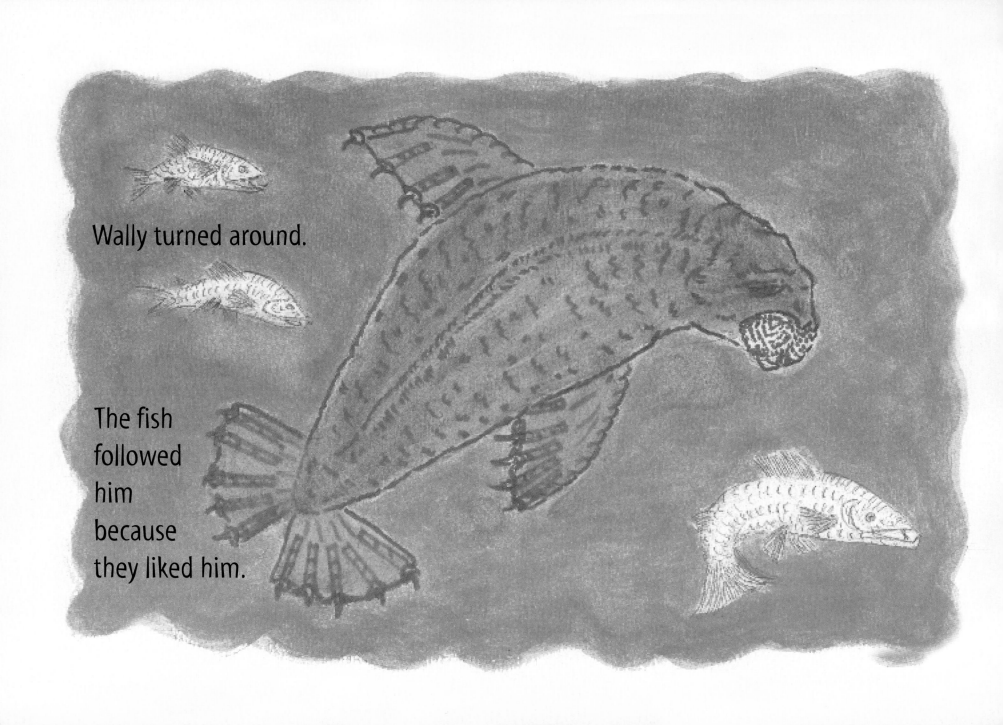

Wally turned around.

The fish
followed
him
because
they liked him.

Wally stopped to rest
on the shore.

He saw two killer whales
swimming near an iceberg.

Wally saw another large
whale swimming in the ocean.

Wally liked his new home.

The Eskimo children loved
to play with him.

He liked the food they
brought him to eat.

Wally was put on iceberg float.
The children made it for him.

The baby walrus enjoyed being in the parade.
He got to see all his friends as he rode by them.

The baby walrus lived there more than a year.

Wally's friends still came to play with him.

He was getting larger with all the good food they fed him.

Wally the lost baby walrus longed for the ocean.

He spent more time out in the Alaska waters.

Wally spotted a herd of walrus swimming close by.

He wanted to join them.

The baby walrus would miss his Eskimo friends if he joined the herd.

Wally must make up his mind what to do.

Wally started to go out into the ocean.

He was soon swimming with them.

Wally was
home at last.

His friends will miss him.

But they know that it is for the best.

Do not worry.

Wally the lost baby walrus
becomes a young adult walrus.

He now lives with the
herd of walrus.

The young walrus soon
starts to grow tusks.

Wally lives happily
ever after!